STARCK

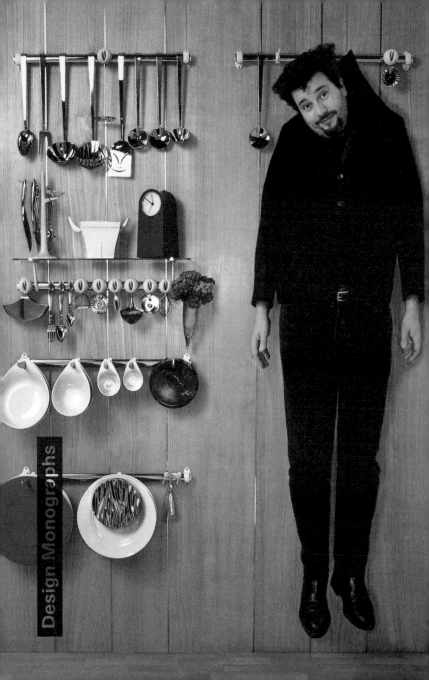

STARCK

JUDITH CARMEL-ARTHUR

Philippe Starck | For more than forty years, Philippe Starck's career has been the subject of a virtual cacophony of accolades. Counted among the best-known and most widely publicized of contemporary international designers, Starck, who was born in Paris on 18 January 1949, was recognized initially for his stylish interiors. A commission in the early 1980s for a redesign of President Mitterrand's private quarters in the Elysée Palace, Paris, catapulted his work into international critical focus. Starck quickly claimed a position as one of the late twentieth century's most prolific and challenging architect-designers and his celebrity status arose as an almost immediate result.

Starck then went on to produce a series of provocative, often luxuriously avant-garde interiors including the Starck Club in Dallas (1984), the Café Costes, Paris (1984; closed 1994), the Manin Restaurant, Tokyo (1987) and the now famous Royalton Hotel, New York (1988). The Café Costes, dominated by its axial, theatrical staircase, and the Royalton, an essay in sheer elegance, invited international attention for their compellingly stylish, postmodern interpretations of interior, public space. Both quickly became pilgrimage sites frequented by devotees of the 1980s designer cult, and set trends within the interior design establishment. Much has been said in the press about Starck's membership in the late twentieth century "cult of celebrity"; and on his ability to capitalize upon this popular, public predilection for urbane elegance. With compliance, he has created environments in which people want to be seen and are seen, proving the ultimate success of his particular version of cosmopolitan spectacle.

But the critical press itself has consistently both aided and abetted Starck's climb to celebrity status. They have, paradoxically, heroized his name itself by

Opposite. Café Costes, Paris, 1984.

recasting it in nimble linguistic variations in order to attract competitive readership. Titles such as "The Art of Starckiness", "Philippe Le Roi", "Starck Contrasts", "Starck Truths", "Starck Lite, Starck Brite", "Starck Staring" and "Starck Treatment" have merely served to exacerbate celebrity, while paralleling Starck's own application of his name to his designs in the 1990s. Among the most effective examples are two garments for Wolford: Starck Naked (1998) and Starck Naked Hot (1999). But numerous other examples arise in the product range covered by the *Good Goods* catalogue (1998), including transport and recreational products such as Kayak Starck (with Rotomod) and Cruiser Starck (with Blauwerk). By means of product names such as these, Starck linguistically consolidates his identity, ensuring his works cannot be verbally recalled without reference to the designer himself. By labelling, he establishes pedigree.

There are a number of notions which can be extracted from Starck's messaging. Labelling is used as a means of focusing upon design origin and provenance. In doing so, Starck celebrates a conceptual triumph of fashion over function, an expression of our current cultural climate. It equally recalls, perhaps, something of Starck's early years (1971–72) as the art director of the Pierre Cardin fashion house in Paris. In the international mass marketing of "designer" goods, the label, often carrying the designer's signature, is worth its weight in gold. Rather than "signing" the outcome of his design endeavours, Starck takes this form of labelling one step further, literally naming the product in his own image. As a marketing strategy, he thus exploits the cult of object labelling to deplete goods of their primary functional significance, translating them into artefacts of private worship and public envy, while simultaneously infusing them with more fantasy than fact. Much as he may choose to deny it, the *Good Goods* catalogue is replete with such aspirational icons of conspicuously "labelled" consumption.

We are working on making things disappear.
Philippe Starck, *LUX*, 2020

Throughout his career, naming has been a consistent postmodernist device used by Starck to invest his products with anthropomorphic qualities, taming them, giving them a somewhat perverse familiarity on the consumer's behalf. Nearly all of his furniture bears quirky names such as Mister Bliss (1982 for XO) and Boom Rang (1992 for Driade), while his product designs have not been spared: Miss Sissi table and wall lamp (1991 for Flos), Jim Nature portable television set (1994 for Saba) and the Moa Moa Bakelite radio (1994 for Telefunken). Some names appear to delightfully honour his children: Ara (the Ara III house boat, and the Ara table lamp of 1988 for Flos) and Oa (the Oa table lamp, 1996 for Flos). Other names are said to derive from the science fiction novels by the author Philip K. Dick: Lola Mundo, Dole Melipone, Tippy Jackson. One way or another, this characteristic combines with the prolific nature of Starck's output to suggest we are meant to recognize in his design "virility" identifiable, named progeny – a Starck "family" – which populates both his world and ours.

It has not been enough that his, on the whole, provocative designs speak for themselves. He has spoken on their and his own behalf, and often. He is perhaps the most interviewed of international design celebrities, having positioned himself as the foremost interpreter of his own work. Of the few books and well over 250 articles that had been written about him by the end of the twentieth century, a good number purported as their "text" somewhat extensive Starck interviews. The designer himself has displaced the journalist, as well as the critic in an attempt by publishers, and Starck himself, to describe high-status, contemporary products and interiors in the "designer's own words", thereby getting closer to "authentic" creative motivation.

Starck's interviews are prescriptive. They are timed and formulated for widespread consumption, and talk of what "good" design should be and what it isn't. Their personal illuminations about individual products and projects reveal something of his design approach, and are thus invaluable sources of information.

They equally demonstrate some of the more intimate aspects of the life behind design. Nevertheless, they should also be seen as self-promotional confessionals aimed directly at the pockets of the Starck consumer. In their frequency and availability in the popular design and home decorating press, such interviews can be argued to not only supplement, but rival the actual purchase of tangible goods in importance. They are moderately priced, saleable commodities meant to complement any toothbrush or plastic chair.

It is fair to say that Starck has tried to generate a genuine discourse between himself and the design world. The personal narrative which his numerous interviews provide emphasizes this, and redresses the absence of equally valuable information within the context of contemporary design where we don't hear nearly enough from designers themselves.

The stylistic background of Starck's design vocabulary is staunchly French, with an informed sprinkling of the Art Deco and the American "streamline" aesthetic of the earlier twentieth century. It must be noted that many of his interior ensembles of the late 1980s, particularly those executed in the United States, can and perhaps should be contextualized within an analysis of images of power in American culture at that time. Nancy Reagan's "politics of symbolism" as outlined by Debora Silverman provided the specific cultural framework for, above all, the interior of Manhattan's Royalton Hotel (1988) and its elegantly manipulative furnishings, including: the high-backed couch, long chair, armchair (all 1991; Driade), the wooden chair of 1988 (Driade) and the Royalton bed (1992; Driade). From the outset the hotel's design agenda was loaded with pre-emptive meaning and quickly became a cultural space frequented by the high-status design consumer and cognoscenti. In this sense it came to function as a proto-sales environment in which the consumer could experience the pleasure and opulence of Starck's furniture and lighting designs first hand. The interiors thus gave the products themselves a cultural status beyond that of the hotel lobby, and one in which any subsequent buyer could share at the moment of purchase.

Starck's interiors at the Royalton very neatly fit into what was then becoming a national, but intrinsically anti-historical "aristocratic" design agenda in America under the Reagan administration, and which had conjoined with a powerful advocacy in the guise of Diana Vreeland's bizarre exhibitions of French decorative design at New York's Metropolitan Museum of Art. Starck was by then France's *enfant terrible* of contemporary design, and would have aroused interest in American high society by participating in the remodelling of President Mitterrand's private apartments earlier in the decade. His interpretations of interior public space at the Royalton as exclusive, feminine, intimate and organic would have evoked a culture of French luxury and pre-Revolutionary social distinction. This would naturally have appealed to the culture of image with its preferences for fantasy illusion which permeated America's "aristocratic" movement of the late 1980s, especially in New York City.

For the domestic landscape Starck has produced self-conscious, commercially high-profile artefacts from multiple media. Objects designed, for example, in the early 1990s for Alessi, are meant for a strictly urban clientele, and are directed towards a comparatively cosmopolitan aficionado whose interest is in enjoying the "spectacle" such objects have to offer. Typical of products arising from this postmodernist domestic agenda, the Max de Chinois colander (1990–91; stainless steel and brass), the Ti Tang teapot (white porcelain with aluminium coating), the Su Mi Tang cream jug (white porcelain) and the Mister Meumeu cheese grater (stainless steel and polyamide),

Below. Hot Bertaa water kettle, 1989, and Juicy Salif citrus squeezer, 1990, both for Alessi.

all dating from 1992, have been infused during the very process of design with a visual language of cultural references. These often witty, certainly multi-layered signifiers, may be more valuable to the consumer than ideas of traditional utility.

Above all, the immensely "masculine" Hot Bertaa kettle (1990–91; plastic and aluminium), an icon of Starck's career and also, by the way, for Alessi, shares significant features with Starck's architecture of the period; including an informed combination of materials, an aggressive architectonic and sculptural quality, the asymmetrical distribution of parts and its stone-like surface treatment, for example: the maquette for the French Pavilion, the Maison de France, 1990, at the Venice Biennale; and the drawings for Star's Door, 1992, Parc de Bercy, Paris. Upon purchase, the consumer is not only buying an Alessi product, but more importantly taking home a little bit of Starck himself; a small portion of his architectural vision of the world.

Objects such as this not only make insistent statements about the continuation of the early twentieth-century "machine" aesthetic in both form and surface treatment, but unite – on behalf of the domestic kitchen – the symbolism of structural technology and metals, on the one hand, with that of expressionist architecture on the other. There is something psychologically bleak here; almost futuristic, but darkly so. The strong sculptural presence of the streamlined "teardrop" shape, a leitmotif of Starck's oeuvre – arguably derived from the influence of American designers – which marks the Hot Bertaa and much of his architecture of the period, also has a metamorphic quality. The forms seem to be emerging from the ground or from the kitchen counter, while the kettle itself is a version upside-down of the subsequent Bordeaux-Mérignac airport project of 1993, a control tower that was a competition design with Luc Arsène-Henry Jr.

Above all, the utility value of the clever Hot Bertaa kettle is truly questionable. It is only ostensibly functional, while clearly exemplifying postmodernist "micro-architecture" for the domestic scene. It was intended to become a design classic and, like kitchen wares produced by Rosenthal of Germany in the 1960s and 1970s, took on immediate design authority by being targeted not towards the consumer, but towards the design museum. Such objects are highly competitive within the kitchenware/ceramics industry for their kudos value, despite the fact that they remain comparatively poor sellers and often don't work.

Here there appears a distinction within Starck's work: objects that could be loosely categorized as the "masculine" or the "feminine". The "feminine" strain is inflected less towards Starck's "masculine", boldly sculptural architectural achievements, than towards his furniture dating from the late 1980s onwards. Much of this shares with his domestic artefacts of approximately the same period a strong biomorphic language of distinctly "feminine" allusions. Sensuous curvilinear forms, evocative organic shapes, and an ethos of intimacy and interiority – of the "salon" – characterize these artefacts in a stereotypically "feminine" manner. Their visual language recalls the naturalistic vocabulary of the eighteenth-century decorative arts in France, and it is no mistake that they also referentially imply the *fin de siècle* Art Nouveau. Starck's national patrimony has provided him with a fertile source of inspiration and quotation, especially within the context of decorative arts history.

Postmodern biomorphism has been regarded as a reaction against the "masculinity" of technology in the waning Machine Age design aesthetic, especially as embodied in the so-called High-Tech style of the 1980s, of which Starck's harshly rectilinear Sarapis stool (1986; tubular steel and steel mesh; Driade) has been considered an example. Biomorphism has been argued to represent a cultural regeneration of a more sensorial "femininity" within the interior landscape. As such it represents an attempt to interject into domestic interiors visually softer, more consumer-friendly products which share the familiar plant, animal and even human forms of their owners and environments. The often witty and playful musings of such domestic objects serve to psychologically invite a wider clientele to purchase, while showing that designers such as Starck are attempting to reintroduce human values into domestic product design.

The President M table of 1981–84 (glass and varnished steel), designed for the bedroom of President Mitterrand's wife in the Elysée Palace, Paris, was among the earliest expressions of biomorphism in Starck's furniture design and may be considered a prefiguration of his later works. The table, which also shows a predilection for simplified and witty structural relationships, was later commercially produced by Baleri for public consumption. The die-cast, fin-like appendages supporting the glass top are notable for their subtle biomorphic configurations, parodying the aerofoils that stabilize rockets, while referencing design history in their play on the American styling used by Raymond Loewy and others of the American streamline aesthetic. Their comparatively small scale, but essential presence in the otherwise High-Tech design is a crucial indicator of Starck's emerging organic tendencies, which ultimately led to the highly sculptural, albeit "feminized" example of the W.W. stool of 1990 (aluminium), produced by Vitra, designed for Wim Wenders, the German film director.

The W.W. stool stands out for its expressive insistence upon the organic. Moreover, like numerous artefacts ultimately bowing to *fin de siècle* France, it acts as a cultural signifier of deeper psychological threads. It talks of impulses of desire – perhaps of purchase – made visible. It hovers uncomfortably between images of dream and those of material reality. The growth metaphor embodied in the forms of the legs and tail of the seat suggests an ongoing debate between reason (function) and emergent emotion (expression). The conscious process of the viewer/user is inhibited from deciding between the two. Interior artefacts such as this undermine any reasoned clarity towards the identity of utilitarian objects, while interjecting a subversive beckoning to the consumer: the hope of transferring from dream into reality the stool's latent embodiment of a domestic "pleasure principle" and all that might imply. In short, the artefact is meant to stimulate the imagination and provoke feelings of desire. It speaks of a late twentieth-century culture of wish-fulfilment.

A series of pieces dating from between those two artefacts shows especially provocative biomorphic and anthropomorphic qualities. These include the Lola Mundo table-cum-chair (1988, cast aluminium and ashwood/ebony finish plywood; Driade); the Louis XX chair (1992, polypropylene and aluminium; Vitra), the Peninsula chair (1995, beechwood with upholstery; XO); Cam El Eon (1999; anodized aluminium and polypropylene/maderon; Driade); and the elegant, stacking chair Olly Tango (1994; chrome tubular steel and bent veneered plywood; Driade).

Opposite. The iconic Louis Ghost chair, here in white enamel at the Quinta do Lago resort in Portugal, Kartell, 2002.

My juicer is not meant to squeeze lemons; it is meant to start conversations.
Philippe Starck, 2004

Varying leitmotifs, some of which seem to behave as dual gender signifiers, fit somewhat uneasily within this category of biomorphic products. The flame, or "streamlined teardrop" motif, said to resemble the wings of a bird or of an aeroplane, has been attributed to paternal influence – Starck's father was an aerodynamics engineer. The theme is as persistent as any within Starck's oeuvre, while its application to as many commercial purposes as possible proves its ability to mutate within Starck's own imagination, multiplying its market potential. The sensuality of the form, its inherent litheness and smooth, erotic curvatures firstly imply the "feminine". This is most apparent in the design of artefacts such as the Laguiole set of stainless steel knives, original design 1986 (manufactured 1996; Alessi); Objets Pointus tableware of 1986 (1996; Alessi); toothbrush and holder, 1989 (manufactured by Fluocaril); O'Kelvin table candlestick in polished turned aluminium and glass, original design 1989 (1996; Alessi); Alo, voice-command telephone 1996 (concept by Starck; design by Jérôme Olivet; Thomson); Vasoo flower vase, 1992 (1996; Alessi) and Hook telephone, 1996 (ABS plastic; Thomson/Alessi).

However, it is typical of Starck to invest his work with multiple references, and a variation on the "flame" theme metamorphoses into an organic, "spermatoid squiggle" whose most notorious manifestation is the rooftop flame of the Asahi Beer Hall in Tokyo of 1990. Its siblings include the Walter Wayle wall clock (1989; thermoplastic resin; Alessi); Sesamo and Apriti door handles (both 1991; aluminium; Ros Kleis); Olympic Flame lighter (1992; stainless steel); Dr Kiss toothbrush (1998; polyamide, Alessi) in which the teasing twist of the tip behaves as a pert welcome.

Starck's ubiquitous "horn" shape is another motif characterized by an inherent cross-gendering. It's simple and elegant formulation in the Ara chrome plated table lamp of 1988 for Flos belies a vision of interiors populated by objects of gentle, feminine curvatures and aggressive, masculine gestures. It is simultaneously one and the same, the dual embodied in the one; unlike the Luci Fair wall sconce (1989; Flos), which is unabashedly phallic in its symbolic implications.

Starck's consistent postmodernist borrowings from diverse sources is a self-conscious mark of his showmanship. The blunted, conical base of the toothbrush for L'Oréal of 1990 acts as a signifier guiding the user/viewer into the realm of sculptural history. The base, or "pedestal", supports what has been rightly argued to be a "Brancusi-like" stem of the toothbrush itself, investing in the design/art-conscious owner a feeling of confident erudition – a reward for recognizing the referential bearings of the object and its quotation from Constantin Brancusi's bronze *Bird in Space* of 1923.

All of these "gendered" pieces bear relationships with the strongly biomorphic statements of Starck's career, often seen in the now famous three-legged chairs of the 1980s and 1990s. An early version (Costes chair, 1982; tubular steel and bent ply shell and leather; Driade) was debuted at the Café Costes, Paris, in 1984, while the motif achieved international acclaim somewhat later in the W.W. stool. It also appeared in the early designs in the Dr Sonderbar chair (1983; tubular steel; XO), the Miss Dorn chair (1982; black fabric, Disform), Ed Archer (cast aluminium and sprung steel; Driade) Pratfall (1987, tubular steel with leather, Driade) and in the Tippy Jackson table (1985; tubular steel and turned steel; Driade). Structurally, the three-legged motif betrays Starck's experimentation with furniture mechanics and his highly regarded, but underplayed genius as a problem-solving technician. In his own right he is a master of rational engineering who is not afraid to negotiate daringly simple solutions; a case in point being the Dole Melipone folding table of 1981 (tubular steel, glass and epoxy; XO).

Starck propagates notions of design as a collective act, and rightly so, but one in which he maintains a creative hierarchy with himself at the top. Previous books on Starck have helped to promote this ideology by including photographic images and portraits of not only Starck and his children, but

Above left. Costes chair, Driade, 1982. **Above right.** La Marie chair, Kartell, 1997.

equally of his friends, collaborators, close associates and patrons, evoking the romance of an extended family. In fact, Starck himself verbally recasts these individuals as his "tribe" in an anthropological posturing. He thus necessarily differentiates between himself together with those who directly support the realization of his personal design agenda, and those who don't. This is tangibly confirmed in the imagery of the chair backs at the Restaurant Felix, Peninsula Hotel (1994, Hong Kong). Each of the Peninsula chairs (1995; XO) boasts the printed, photographic portrait of one of the tribe members, including Starck's daughter Ara, his then-fiancée Patricia Bailer, and a portrait of Starck himself. This form of homage to his nearest and dearest is also a gesture of objectification. The tribe becomes something which is at once personalized and marketable. This is a comparatively opulent expression of familial heroism. The aristocracy of design becomes the design itself, and is absorbed into the mechanisms of consumption. Consumers are not the beneficiaries of this mythology, but victims reciprocally defined as "outside" the tribe until they are able to participate in its legacy by buying into the Starck range.

This is Starck at his most subtle, but least ambivalent. A number of interviews with the designer in the last decade of the twentieth century fell victim to proclamations of his disdain for the label-conscious, materialistic 1980s. In its place, Starck proposed a "new" emphasis on what he termed "democratic high fashion"; that is, high-quality, tasteful industrial design available to everyone. Unfortunately, this proposition lacks originality in its basic premise, blatantly harking back to the design principles of the Bauhaus and beyond that to the Deutscher Werkbund.

Within this context the 1998 *Good Goods* catalogue was a self-conscious marketing gesture, but one in which Starck redefined the role of the turn-of-the-millennium designer as that of paternalist whose task is both to guard and enrich society with his store of home-grown truths and environmentally friendly products.

Not all the catalogue's products were designed by Starck himself, but all of the approximately 200 items were included under his immediate auspices. The catalogue opened with a selection of organic foods, including wine, basmati rice, spaghetti, biscuits and organic champagne produced by OAO. Then came a selection of eco-clothing; wardrobe prototypes "already familiar to the collective memory" and available in basic colours only. All the garments boasted a No Creation, No Chemical mark, woven of organically grown cotton and containing a politically correct, promotional tagging.

The 9 months T-shirts designed by Patricia Bailer were the cleverest and indeed the most saleable of this lot, while the rain gear, albeit functional, urban and "properly" synthetic, served largely once again to ennoble the designer himself with titles such as: Wet Angel Starck, Wet Duke Starck and Wet Elegance Starck. In addition to shampoos, creams, fly swats, cutlery, appliances, linens and a new range of Starck paints, the catalogue offered little more than a selection of comparatively more affordable Starck classics such as the Miss Sissi lamp manufactured by Flos (1991), an array of well- and slightly lesser-known Alessi products (e.g. Dr Cheese toothbrush, 1998), the Ola telephone by Thomson (1996), and the ubiquitous Excalibur loo brush (1993, Heller). One of Starck's chairs then new to the market, La Marie (1997, Kartell), was shown to advantage within an assortment of easily manufactured and therefore affordable plastic household artefacts which also included

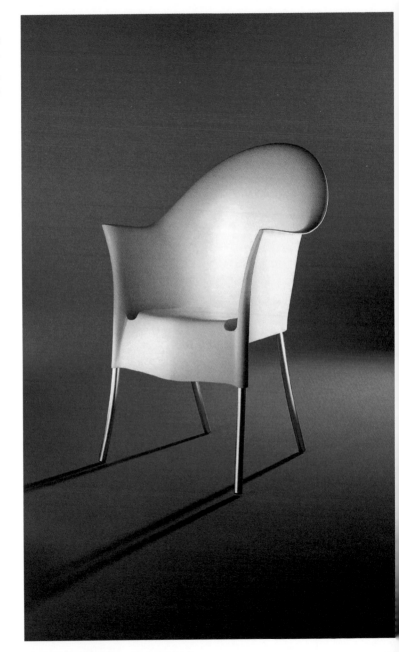

varieties of the Lord Yo (produced by Fedra, 1994) and Cheap Chic (XO, 1996) chairs, and the Prince Aha stool (Kartell, 1996). Two of the most politically compelling items available for sale through the catalogue were the Respirator with three separate filters (both normal- and large-capacity for chemical impurities, and one "dust and particle filter including radiological dust"), and the now infamous Teddy Bear Band which sported a head-like, cuddly-toy mutation on all but one of its appendages.

Taken overall, the *Good Goods* catalogue was a mission statement; a political mandate encouraging fidelity, family values, home decoration and the pursuit of the clean life, in addition to an apocalyptic vision of self-protection against all invading impurities, including the socio-political, if not ethnic "other". As a transparent marketing strategy it was immensely politically correct. It was unequivocally directed towards the middle classes whose political and economic bearings are such that they would decode its hidden assumptions and comprehend its neo-conservative messaging. In *Good Goods*, Starck expressed a series of socio-economic stereotypes and propagated the notion that what is good for them is something he would supply, or something that could be supplied under his tutelage. In the introduction to the catalogue, he claimed to interrogate the basic terms by which we culturally construct relationships between products and consumers, but because of the strategic bias of the catalogue his wasn't an efficient argument.

Whatever its objective effectiveness at fulfilling its remit, the *Good Goods* catalogue certainly established a template for Starckian product design in the twenty-first century. Environmentally sensitive projects, embracing durable and recyclable materials, along with a general decluttering, became the order of the day.

A string of seating projects embody this trend. In 2000, Stark reimagined Emeco's classic Navy chair – originally created in 1944 for the US Navy – in recycled aluminium. Two years later, the million-selling Louis Ghost chair for Kartell took the original Louis XVI design from the eighteenth century and reconceived it *sans* joinery, polycarbonate plastic from a single mould. It was

Opposite. Lord Yo chair, Driade, 1994.

originally produced in a see-through finish, the better to chime with the designer's ongoing efforts to do away with distracting elements in a piece. "When waiting for certain objects to disappear," he has commented (in reference to paring away unnecessary features from designs), "they have to be rendered bearable by a choice of view coming from an attempt at invisibility through transparency."

As part of the process, established industrial designs have been re-dressed in more ecologically friendly attire. The Miss Sissi lamp was reproduced in 2016 in 100 per cent naturally biodegradable plastic – created from sugar beet and sugar-cane waste – courtesy of Flos and the biotech company Bio-on, while in 2012 Emeco remade Starck's stackable Broom chair with discarded lumber and plastic. Starck has persisted with synthetics when he felt that their cost would be outweighed by using natural materials, however, even though the choice might prompt criticism in some quarters. "I prefer to work with fossil energy than to cut down trees," he told *LUX* in 2020, "and I would rather use vinyl for upholstery than kill cows."

As part of his ongoing investigation into biodegradable and sustainable materials, Starck collaborated with Cassina in 2019 on the experimental Croque la Pomme, a set of sixteen pieces of furniture covered in Apple Ten Lork vegan fabric – leather sourced from apple cores and skins – available in white, black or orange. To announce its arrival, Cassina's Rive Gauche showroom in Paris was reconfigured to accommodate an installation referencing three cultural touchstones for the fruit: the story of Adam and Eve, Newton's development of the theory of gravity and Rene Magritte's iconic

As far as interior design is concerned, everything will disappear slowly: curtains shall be replaced by liquid crystal windows.
Philippe Starck, *Dazed Digital*, 2010

Surrealist work *The Son of Man* (1964), wherein a green apple substitutes for the subject's facial features.

In another innovative milestone, Starck partnered with Kartell later that same year to produce the A.I. chair. The seat utilized 100 per cent recycled thermoplastic technopolymer – redeploying clean industrial waste and reducing the emissions involved in the production process. Even more significantly, Starck worked with software specialists Autodesk to engineer a radical new approach to its formation: "generative design", in which artificial intelligence works towards an optimum design that meets all the requirements inputted by a designer or engineer, including choice of materials, budgetary limits and manufacturing process (in this case, injection moulding). Over time (in this case, three years), the system acquires understanding of the desired aesthetic and penchants, and can even anticipate them – to the extent that in 2021 Starck himself assured *Purple* magazine that it was the system that designed the chair, not himself. (In a theme that we'll revisit later, he also commented on the smooth "organic" lines of the piece, which he compared to those of plants – but which implicitly also bring to mind the hallmarks of classic Art Nouveau style.)

For the man whose mind seems to be as inquisitively open as ever now that he is in his seventies, this heralds a new dawn. "AI is going to create a new freedom in design," he assured *LUX* in 2010. With a Rimbaud-like disavowal of past certainties, he insisted, "Design as we know it will be dead. There will be better solutions to sitting down than a chair." And for this perpetually questioning creator, AI's advantages are not limited to product design, but must be hard-wired into the future of the human race itself. "The only way to pursue our evolution is to realize the dream we have of ourselves, the dream of the new human," he advised *Purple*, adding – perhaps for reassurance – "artificial intelligence is never anything but an extension of our intelligence."

Many of Starck's past high-profile designs had been criticized for favouring cachet over functionality (exhibit A: the divisive Juicy Salif lemon squeezer), or prohibitive price tags. Yet the new century found him increasingly prioritizing affordability and utility. His reference to himself as a Robin Hood of the design world may initially appear idiosyncratically tongue-in-cheek, or even offensive, but he's made it a practice frequently to adapt his luxury projects, by means of using more cost-effective materials, for those with shallower pockets. ("I do use such projects like a lab," he insisted to *Die Zeit* in 2008.) It epitomizes the so-called "democratization" of design that Starck helped pioneer in the early 1980s – understandably so, given the fetishization of elitism and edition pieces in the design world at the time. In fact, it places him within a laudable tradition of visionary groups and individuals whose guiding principle was to make good design available to all, from the Bauhaus to Habitat founder Terence Conran – who also masterminded London's Design Museum, making thought-provoking design readily available to the public.

Perhaps this implies a subtle evolution of Starck's overarching philosophy. In the past, he sought to inject a note of off-kilter humour and pleasure into the domestic environment with his aesthetic, but the new century finds him broadening his outlook into that of a fully fledged existentialist designer, to whom the ecological impact of production processes, along with a product's longevity and its place in creating a happier human future, all become watchwords. The Starckian "family" had once implied a coterie of in-the-know, like-minded aesthetes who instinctively "got" the designer's message, his imprimatur its guarantee. But over the past twenty years, Starck has become increasingly vocal about expanding his tribe to include all of humanity, and taken intriguing steps towards improve its welfare.

Ever the iconoclast, Starck himself envisages a future becoming ever-more streamlined, a vision already well underway in a world of cloud storage, wireless technology and streamed entertainment. "Future is about dematerialization," he insisted in 2010. "Dematerialization is in fact one of my main focuses: you can see it in the Louis Ghost chair, in the elegance of minimalism in my watches." A future, indeed, that – in light of developments in generative design – may have no need for designers as we understand the term today. (That said, the man who told *Dazed Digital* "I have no desire to develop more products" in 2010, hasn't stopped developing them.)

That less-is-more aesthetic inhabits the clean lines of the Starck V basin mixer (2014; glass, chrome; Axor). It's there too in the Aeklys smart ring (2020; ABS and TPU plastics with NFC chip; ICARE Technologies). The device allows for contactless payments and access to public transportation, but with a raft of potential add-ons, including integration into management of smart homes

A house should not cost more than a car.
Philippe Starck, *'A'A'*, 2021

– paring away the need for extraneous facets of one's life as Starck himself might prune unnecessary features from a design.

In 1969, hitherto a somewhat directionless student at the École Nissim de Camondo, Starck had created an inflatable structure for Perce-Neige, an organization that catered for physically and mentally handicapped individuals. Set in the entrance to the Grand Palais, it had created a buzz, garnering Starck national news coverage and a renewed sense of focus. Fast forward to 2014, and he was making headlines again for what was touted as Europe's first inflatable private building – health and wellbeing centre Le Nuage in Montpellier – whose exterior was wrapped in giant inflated polymer bubbles, admitting plentiful light but obscuring those inside from the prying gaze of passers-by.

The Dial for SNSM (2018; silicone with inbuilt GPS tracker; ido-data) took the concept of a design for life quite literally – a sleek, flexible smart wristband that can contact rescue services, or one's family or friends, if the user experiences problems at sea. Developed in tandem with France's emergency-rescue organization Les Sauveteurs en Mer (SNSM), the waterproof device emits a regular reading of the user's location, crucially enabling rescuers to reach the site as soon as possible. Currently retailing at 169 euros, it is also more modestly priced than many of Starck's iconic products. In 2011, he'd carped to Spear's that, "Twenty years ago it was perhaps a little funny to lose time speaking about the beauty of the lamp. Now it's an obscenity. Because design doesn't save life." With Dial, he'd perhaps come close to resolving his own complaint.

The theme fragility of life serves as the setting for one of the most arresting of Starck's early twenty-first-century works. It's characteristic that the creator of some of the most highly prized (and often prohibitively priced) designs of the past forty years, and whose visionary imagination has turned luxury hotels across the globe into fantasy worlds and turned out super yachts such as Steve Job's *Venus* (unveiled a year after the owner passed), should also be capable of delivering the odd shock. He's described himself as "subversive, ethical, ecological, political, humorous," and most of those adjectives could equally be applied to 2005's startling Gun lighting collection for Flos. Take the stand of the table lamp, a gold-plated likeness of a Kalashnikov AK47 topped off with a black lampshade, inside which black crosses serve as reminders of the departed. Gold and black; money and death. And while the price tag might cause cynics to roll their eyes, it's worth remembering that 20 per cent of sales from the range go to the NGO Frères des Hommes, which is active in developing countries bedevilled by conflict.

Those pining for the playful Philippe Starck who – notably in collaboration with Ian Schrager – created hotels with an outsized, fantasy element to them, beginning with Times Square's Royalton – can still find traces of him in more recent architectural projects. His renovations for Paris's Le Royal Monceau hotel (originally an Art Deco belle of the jazz age) kicked off with a VIP-

Below. Gun lamps, Flos, 2005.

studded, DJ-soundtracked "demolition party' in 2008. Two years later, the results were unveiled: ultra-luxe understated elegance alongside Starckian interventions with a twist of *Alice in Wonderland*. Inspired by the gentleman adventurer, writer and collector André Malraux, rooms bear enticing mementoes of imaginary past residents (love letters stuffed in drawers, a string of pearls here, a signed guitar there) and wry touches: room 581's writing desk sports a top set at a deliberately off-kilter angle, and each room has its own bad-taste artwork.

Consider, too, what's in the pipeline: the fourteen-storey Maison Heler hotel for the Hilton Group in Metz, its monolithic structure surmounted by a traditional eighteenth-century-style Alsatian house, complete with garden and a tree at each corner. "Phantasmagoric" – Starck's own description – feels entirely apt. And scheduled to open in 2023 at the LA Organic agritourist outpost on the outskirts of Ronda in southern Andalusia, LA Almazara – a cubic mill/museum dedicated to the history and culture of olive oil production, its exterior is broken by a thrusting horn (shades of that phallic Luci Fair wall sconce for Flos) – constructed by submarine manufacturers – which has seen this obstinate brutalist block ("totally out of scale," Starck cheerfully confesses) dubbed "El Toro". The walls also feature a twelve-ton olive and a giant eye motif in the style of Pablo Picasso, which billows smoke; behind it is a fireplace. Starck is creative director and a co-founder; tellingly, he insisted that the produce be organic and pesticide-free when he came on board in the early 1990s.

Starck's understanding of the impact of understatement bears fruition in the sleek wine cellar for the Château les Carmes Haut-Brion estate, completed in 2016. It was the result of a partnership with architect and friend, Luc Arsène-Henry Jr, who describes it "as a blade fallen from the sky", although a ship's prow is an equally appropriate comparison, given the historical maritime export of Bordeaux wines. That placement makes sense when one understands that the four-level structure is located near to the heart of the port city, making it imperative that the vat house and gravity-fed barrel cellar within are kept environmentally stable.

In the field of architecture too, the importance of design that is affordable as well as innovative has become imperative to this multi-faceted designer.

In the beginning, computers were big as a house. Now there are computers in the size of only a credit card. In ten years from now they are going to be in our bodies – bionics. In fifty years from now, the concept of computers will have dematerialized itself.
Philippe Starck, *Die Zeit*, 2008

With 2014's Prefabricated Accessible Technological Homes (P.A.T.H.), he partnered with Riko to create affordable wooden prefab housing. Quick to assemble, and designed to integrate heat pumps, solar panels, wind turbines and rainwater collectors, they offered a cost-effective, green alternative to an overheated and increasingly unaffordable global housing market. Crucially, given contemporary ructions in the global energy markets, they also offer the possibility of generating more energy than they consume.

Of his more recent projects, one of the most novel is his work on the habitation module on the first commercial space station, to be built and operated by Axiom Space, using a port on the International Space Station. Starck's interiors convey a worm-like warmth, with an array of LED lights that flux in accordance with the inhabitants' biorhythms and moods.

The space taken up by the human body remains an ongoing field of investigation for this polymath talent. In the third decade of the twenty-first century, Starck continues to focus on his concept of "bionism" – design inspired by organic forms to create a more refined technology better suited to humans. ("There's nothing more economical than nature," he told *Purple* magazine in 2021.) The Starck Eyes spectacles (a collaboration with confrère

Alain Mikli, later rebranded as Starck Biotech Paris) incorporate a screwless hinge whose 360-degree movement was styled after the ball-and-socket joint in the shoulder. And over a series of collaborations with Ipanema that began in 2015, he worked towards producing a sandal that could replicate as closely as possible the sensation of walking barefoot; its genesis was as streamlined as the footwear itself, with 100 per cent recyclable materials and a production process adapted to become more manual and less industrial. The genesis of both projects reflects Starck's insistence that "The closer you get to the body, the less you can lie." That statement carries more than a dusting of moral philosophy, something that regularly emerges in Starck's interviews – witness his comment (in the context of the *Good Goods* catalogue) in 2010 that "Hopefully, people will start understanding what they are offered and asking themselves 'Do I need to buy this product?' I think refusal is the first good act."

And from creating products that feel as if they're part of the body, it's a short step (or a brief sketch on the designer's bespoke weather- and humidity-resistant tracing-paper pad) to incorporating them corporeally.

Is Starck's insistence that he had sought to destroy design, and had accomplished that feat, or that "Everything I have created is absolutely unnecessary. Design ... is absolutely void of usefulness" (as he informed *Die Zeit*) simply waggish perversity? Or breath-taking clarity in a self-destructively over-materialistic world? Or perhaps it's simply proof that the lone term "designer" cannot encapsulate what Philippe Starck is all about: that his core design project remains nothing less than the refinement of human life itself.

Overleaf. Philippe Starck in the Eurostar lounge he designed at Waterloo Station, London, 2002.

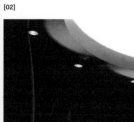

[01, 02, 03, 04, 05, 06] Royalton Hotel and interior, New York City, 1988.

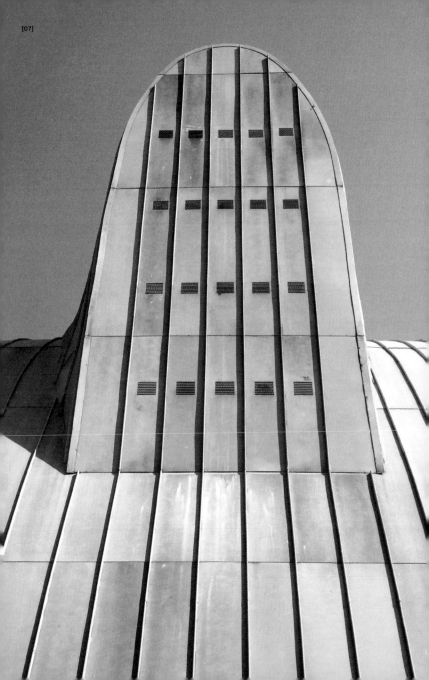

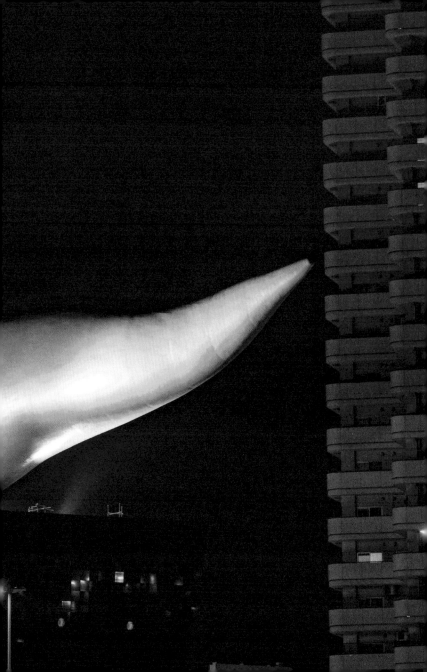

[07, 08] Unhex Nani Nani Building, Tokyo, 1989; [09, 10, 11] Asahi Beer Hall, Tokyo, 1990;
[12] Paramount Hotel, New York City, 1990; [13, 14] Felix Restaurant and Oyster Bar,
Peninsula Hotel, Kowloon, 1994; [15, 16, 17] Delano Hotel and interior, Miami, 1995.

1m35

[18] St Martin's Lane Hotel, London, 1999; [19] Kong Restaurant, Paris, 2003; [20] Lan Lounge Bar, Hangzhou, 2007; [21] Ramses Restaurant, Madrid, 2008; [22] Raffles, Le Royal Monceau, Paris, 2010.

[23] Le Nuage, Montpellier, 2014; [24, 25] P.A.T.H. (Prefabricated Accessible Technological Homes) project, 2014 to present; [26] Le Meurice, Paris, 2016; [27] wine cellar, Château les Carmes de Haut-Brion, 2016; [28, 29] Hotel Brach, Paris, 2018; [30] Café Ha(a)ïtza, 2015, and [31] La Co(o)rniche, 2010, Arcachon.

[32]

[33]

[34]

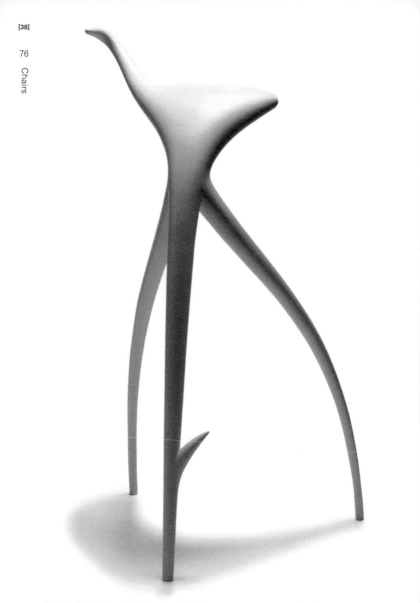

[32] Dr Sonderbar chair, XO, 1983; [33] Costes chair, Driade, 1982; [34] Miss Dorn chair, Disform, 1982; [35] Sarapis bar stool, Driade, 1986; [36, 37] Dr Glob chair, Kartell, 1988; [38] W.W. stool, Vitra, 1990; [39] BuBu stool, XO, 1991.

[40] Dr No chair, Kartell, 1996; [41] Cheap Chic chair, XO, 1996; [42] Prince Aha stool, Kartell, 1996; [43] BuBu stool, XO, 1991; [44] La Marie chair, Kartell, 1997; [45] Toy chair, Driade, 1999; [46] Navy chair, Emeco, 2000; [47] Louis Ghost chair, Kartell, 2002.

[48] Masters chair, Kartell, 2005; **[49]** Zartan chair, Magis, 2012; **[50]** A.I. chair, Kartell, 2019; **[51]** Adela Rex armchair, Andreu World, 2021; **[52]** Broom chair, Emeco, 2012.

Slick Slick by S+ARCK 1999

red by Parrot

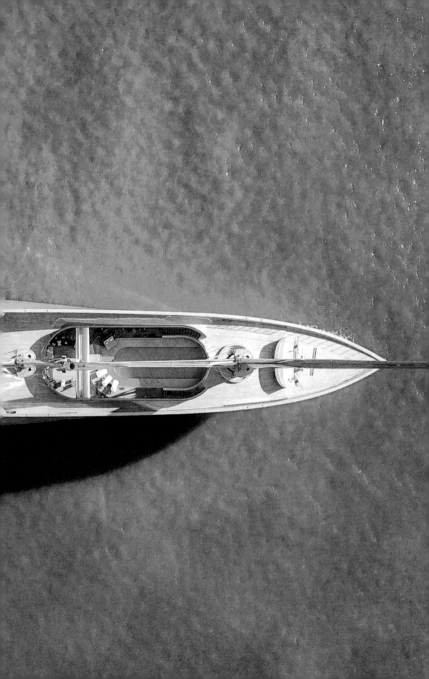

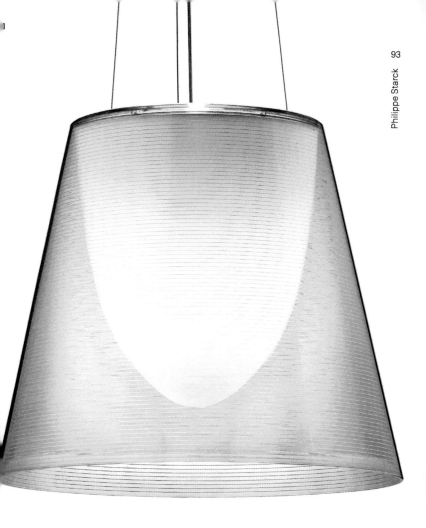

[53] Dr NA table, Kartell, 1997; [54] Tronc tables, XO, 2008; [55] Sailing Yacht A, Nobiskrug, 2015; [56] Miss Sissi lamps, Flos, 1991; [57] KTribe S3 lamp, Flos, 2005.

[58] Miss K table lamp, Flos, 2003; [59] Gun lamp, Flos, 2005.

[60] Hot Bertaa kettle, Alessi, 1987; [61] Juicy Salif lemon squeezer, Alessi, 1990;
[62] Ti Tang teapot, Alessi, 1990; [63] Mister Meumeu grater, Alessi, 1992;
[64] Faitoo Mangetoo cutlery, Alessi, 1996; [65] Excalibur loo brush, Heller, 1993.

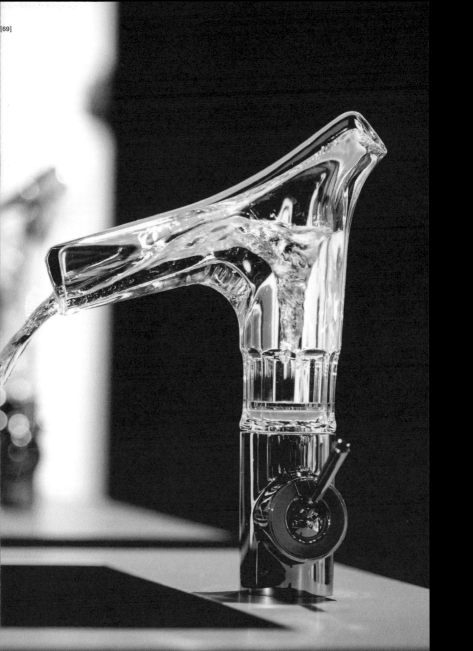

Philippe Starck

[66] Dr Spoon, Alessi, 1998; [67] Dr Kiss, Alessi, 1998; [68] St Martin's Hotel bathroom, London, 1999; [69] Starck V basin mixer, Axor, 2014; [70] Jim Nature TV, Saba, 1994; [71] Dr Skud fly swatter, Alessi, 1998.

Picture Credits

The publishers would like to thank the following sources for their kind permission to reproduce the pictures in this book.

Alamy /A. Astes 89/Andreas von Einsiedel 15, 54, 100b/Andy Stagg-VIEW 38, 39/Avalon.red 18r, 83/Chris Willson 11/Digitalman 62/Directphoto Collection 55/dpa picture alliance 101/EyeEm 84/Hemis 4–5, 56–61, 64–5, 70, 71/Hugh Threlfall 94/Kazimierz Jurewicz 74/Photo Japan 42–3/redsnapper 81/Steve Speller 79/Viennaslide 7. **Alessi s.p.a** 2, 96, 100tl, 100tr. **Arcaid** /Earl Carter/ Belle 48, 49, 50–3/David Churchill 46–7/Richard Bryant 5, 32–7/Simon Kenny /Belle 48, 49. **Brach/EVOK Collection** 68, 69. **Emeco** 87bl, 87br. **Flos Ltd** 26, 92, 93, 95. **Getty Images** /Alain Jocard 110b/Gerry Penny 30–1/Mehdi Fedouach 66–7/Miguel Medina 87t. **Jean Baptise Mondina/Wolford** 104–5. **Kartell** 86. **Magis** /Tom Vack 85. **Purves & Purves** 99. **Saba Personal Electronics** 102. **Shutterstock** /Edward O'Neil 82/pio3 44–5/Pisit Kitireungsang 40–1/StockStudio Aerials 90–1. **S+ARCK** /Network 18l, 20, 110t/with Riko (www.starckwithriko.com) 63/with Ipanema 106–7. **Welbeck Publishing Group** /Matthew Ward 72, 73, 75–8, 80, 88, 97, 98, 103.

Every effort has been made to acknowledge correctly and contact the source/ copyright holder of the images. Welbeck Publishing Group apologizes for any unintentional errors or omissions which will be corrected in future editions of this book.

[72] Wolford dresses by Starck, 1998 and 1999; [73] Ipanema footwear, 2015; [74] Pibil city bike, Peugeot, 2013; [75] LED watch, Fossil, 2000; [76] Aeklys One smart ring, 2020.

First published in 1999.

This revised and updated edition published in 2023 by OH! Life
An imprint of Welbeck Non-Fiction Limited, part of Welbeck Publishing Group.
Based in London and Sydney.
www.welbeckpublishing.com

Text and Design © Welbeck Non-Fiction Limited 1999, 2023
Cover image: Masters chair by Philippe Starck. Courtesy Kartell.

A CIP catalogue record for this book is available from the British Library.

ISBN 978-1-83861-114-9

Associate publisher: Lisa Dyer
Contributing writer: Rob Dimery
Design: www.gradedesign.com
Production controller: Felicity Awdry

Printed and bound in China

10 9 8 7 6 5 4 3 2 1